Work by Bloodlight

Work by Bloodlight

Poems

Julia Bouwsma

Winner of the 2015 *Cider Press Review* Book Award

Cider Press Review
San Diego

Cider Press Review
PO BOX 33384
San Diego, CA, USA
CIDERPRESSREVIEW.COM

First edition
10 9 8 7 6 5 4 3 2 1 0

ISBN: 9781930781238
Library of Congress Control Number: 2016958949

Cover photo: William Blake, *Satan Smiting Job with Sore Boils*. Ca. 1826. Photo image courtesy Tate, London / Art Resource, NY. *This work is in the public domain.*
Author photograph by Margot Cochran
Cover and book design by Caron Andregg

ABOUT THE CIDER PRESS REVIEW BOOK AWARD:

The annual *Cider Press Review* Book Award offers a $1,500 prize, publication, and 25 author's copies of a book-length collection of poetry. For complete guidelines and information, visit CIDERPRESSREVIEW.COM/ BOOKAWARD.

Printed in the United States of America
at Bookmobile, Minneapolis, MN

Contents

Not a cruel song, no, no, not cruel at all. This song
Is sweet. It is sweet. The heart dies of this sweetness.

—Brigit Pegeen Kelly

Spell for Spring

When you hear the woodcock's nasal *peent*—drop trees across that gravel
gully you call road. Drag limbs to the smolder fire. Your land swells now
with peels, grinds, shells, as sweet as condemnation, sin. The cat fetches
you a flying squirrel, half carcass on the front porch seeping rain—
in the path you will find a long green hairpin with a glass jewel for an eye.
Now the ground burbles song over your boots. Come closer.
A cluster fly drowns in the sap pail. Now you will crave
the taste of dirt under your fingernails. In your teeth. Throat.
You will learn to swallow your hands.

Pariah's Call

Little hand, how I fled to the woods is a story you think you know:
the sweet rotting scent of the shed out back, relentless birdsong
a dome on the sky, how shade-trees cloister the skin and sunlight
bleaches the eyes. Something soured in me so long, soft whiskeyed teeth
could not chew; taste of flesh gave way to spreading stain. Mud cut
through hilltop, the washed out road I walk in spring, where
will shame not find me? Little hand, you think you know—

First Words

Because I was still inside my mother. Because my father was in the middle
of a field, searching for a four-leaf clover so I could be born. Because he
spent weeks on his hands and knees, hunting. Because one night,
right before it got dark—when it's hardest to see—he finally found it.
Because that night, I was born.

Or try it this way: once upon a time, there was an elf who worked
as a cowherd, telling the cows which clover was poisonous.
But he wanted to go to The Great Festival. So he fashioned a white stamp
and stamped all the edible clover, saying to the cows,
You must eat only that which bears the white mark on its leaves.
Then he left. For three days it rained. The white ink bled.
When the elf returned, he found every clover awash in white.

Because this is how you mark a child, make her yours
forever. Press your story like a blessing
into her still-bruised forehead.

If I tell you all the stories, how will you know
which ones are true—which you can eat, which ones
will eat you?

Out of the Lockbox

Athena speaks to Erichthonius

We both know what it is to hide. As a child you had soft teeth, a tongue
that wouldn't lie flat, couldn't stay down—always ready to escape
from the wooden chest, the casket, the lockbox. I took a string. I hung
our fate around your neck: a drop from the first vial would ferment
your blood; a drop from the second—you might live forever.

Those prying bitches screamed, riding their skirts as they fell from turrets:
the oldest first, the youngest next. After you were betrayed, you snuggled in
with the snakes at my breast. I felt like a mother. I glanced down at you
and you gazed up. Rest found on Medusa's stiff, severed head.
And when you closed your eyes and went to sleep, your face was still
as your pillow—the bulging bone of your half sister I'd cursed.
That day I set you down, I had to raise my shield. I turned away.
I had to. How could I afford that tenderness?

For the Beaver Hanging in My Shed

Soft brown albatross, you have been with me all winter,
hanging upside down from your gambrel of twine. Your flank
still stabbed with pliers that twist back fur, expose
a pink slice of flesh. Frozen for months, you will thaw now
and fill my shed with your smell. Back claws black,
long broken fingers—*how I swerved right for you*—now
extended and searching for air as front nails glisten
blood, dark bead uncurling the stained grain bag on the floor.
Tail bent to the wire stretched at the base of the gambrel,
mouse pellets in the hollow between your legs.
The slit down your chest is a faint seam of fur:
tufts of white down shedding guard hairs, bristling brown light,
ears pasted wet to the head. How fat you are with hanging!
Swollen gut sagging, fluid draining thick and purple,
pooling the sack below. Outside, snow slides off the roof—

the ground is bloating. Sunlight catches blood as it drips.
You were all winter swiveling silent in the dark. It's March
before I come to write you to life, and already you are rotting
yourself back. Soft brown friend, what does it matter
that I didn't kill you myself? Both our tongues have crusted shut.
What's underneath is thick sediment, rich dark loam;
newly-hatched flies circle. I pry open our mouths.

Origin Story

In my dreams, lagoons. I swim through them alone, in clothes. This water,
dark as spilled ink. My father is afraid of water. What I remember most—
the silent paleness of his stomach, the three black hairs that rose
near his navel. My father, he fears leeches and invertebrates. *Your birth
was a last ditch attempt to save the marriage,* he tells me. The water is warm
from the bodies before mine. I swim off to find those bodies
but find only crowded clots of rotten leaves. My father, he fears
the sight of his own feet, how they stretch and curl beneath waves,
that webbed rippling of a stillborn. It is an odd truth
that underwater survival depends on losing
the desire to breathe.

A Taxidermist Demands Accountability

This is the art of preparing, stuffing, mounting. Let's display
my skin. I'll watch you look inside. Stretch your hide
around the fact: you aren't the only one. Last week
I wished to be hollow—a gutted weasel, dried
and worn as a puppet around your index finger.
Today I want to line up shots of formaldehyde on the bar
and make you drink them to remember. Only liars
don't eat meat. I want to skin it all in front of you, stitch
my memory over yours, see you flinch. This denial makes me
sick. Yesterday a Pennsylvania woman climbed into her bathtub
with her young sons and sat on them. She kept her clothes on.
Sometimes the voices chant nothing but *drown drown
drown,* and we do it to drown them out. Preservation exists
in so many forms. Mummified in cellophane; strapped to
Styrofoam trays. Carcass in plaster. Carcass removed.
These days, you don't have to slit the body cavity.
Glass eye, fake teeth, tongue. I bet you like it clean like that.

We Are Just Three Mouths

A rifle on my shoulder, I am in the henhouse again.
The scream is one pitch too high for human. The weasel
is a white scarf at her throat, pas de deux of feather and fur
I watch through my gunsight, empty metal eye
inches from its collar of snow, blast that shatters any dance.
The weasel falls back, starts to rise, as if it were easy, one motion,
no difference between the hen's blood in its mouth and the red
hole spreading its ribs. I step on it hard: the flash of black eyes.
It claws, bites my boot. We are three bodies in soiled pine shavings,
three mouths. The weasel winces, eyes close, open—limbs stretch
into the last hard act of breath. The second bullet slips,
trembling, from my hand. I drop the gun hard, once. Twice.
But the weasel's elegant neck won't snap. I find the bullet,
reload, press into the pink-white fold of ear, pull.
Gunpowder in sawdust, a soft head slap. I reach down
to grasp what I have done. I lift it by the tail.

When to Dispatch

When it finds its way into the henhouse, when it quills the dog,
when she snags her leg in the fence and the others
smell her blood before you do, when it gnaws the siding
off your house at 3 AM, when it builds its dam in the road,
when you crush his hindquarters with your car,
when she births her calf then lies head lolling into the grass
too weak to stand, too weak to nurse, after three days,
when it won't eat, won't drink, won't lay, when an ear flick
no longer holds off flies, when there's cancer
in the bone, in the heart, when ribs snap, when lungs
puncture, when the tail uncurls, when he breaks his back, barn straw
clinging as he stumbles up the hill to sleep on your porch,
when it's bleeding in your bathtub, after a week, after he pisses himself,
pisses blood, when it comes to you on three legs,
when she wants to die at your feet, when he tries to bite back.
Then you step into night, gather strength
to the back of your hand, already the warm heft of *now*
slung over your shoulder. Then you get your gun.

Elegy as Now

Finally, I wash the dishes. I am drizzling soap
into yogurt containers when you come in, the spotted salamander
on your glove. *I found him in the grave.* The salamander stares at me, eyes
the blackest beads I've ever seen. You set it in the brown bowl
on the table, a splash of water. I use the steamer basket for a lid.
I want to keep the salamander and name it after the dog.
You go back out to dig more grave, to make it *a little longer.*
I will keep washing dishes.

Following the Snare-Line

A poem, spoken aloud, rises up in mid-flight and crashes down
into a child's skull, flattening itself against the pillow-creased face
of her nightmares. Reverberate—it's that early morning light
of first memory, gray twist of promise that can't be trusted.
A window screen is left ajar. A trail of footprints glistens
along pine floors, tint of blood. The air is July-cut grass,
but outside snow congeals yellow as bear fat. The child presses
forehead to glass door. Out in the woods, behind the house:
a trap, a blackened clot of fur swinging from sagging maple.
She follows the dream down the hall—the trail winds silently,
stops in front of the closed door. The child waits, smudges plaster
with her cracked palms, stains the doorknob with her breath.
One voice still bellows inside her head: sings one poem into another.
The dream's footsteps force the door ajar. Inside, their mouths
will be as slack and white as sheets, their limbs snapping awake
as they fall toward her. This repetition will steam the air
again and again like smoke.

We Go on Vacation; the Calligrapher Stays Home

The first night alone, he drives down the hill then idles his car
in front of the Basset Street School where the face at his window asks,
White or red? He stammers, *Weed*—but drives home, meek, with a baggy
of coke, which he cuts on the counter beside his mouse pad
and snorts through a half-formed calligraphy pen. The brass cylinder
rolls to the floor. The sound of its arc scraping the wood is a motion his fingers
absorb until, at last, he finds himself drawing fast. Catching sight
of his face in the computer screen, he traces the shadows that glimmer
his jaw. Letters align tendon to muscle, angled juncture of joint and bone,
until the birds begin to sing louder than the lines can shine in his head,
until the cramped hand becomes a knotted fist that no longer obeys—
then he paces the narrow pine of the studio, licking his lips to taste
what he so recently owned. He creaks through the house
room by room. Mine is last: the patterns I see when I sleep: his weight
against the rumpled folds, the ink-stained quilts my aunt sewed.
He closes his eyes in my empty bed.

The Leech Child

I was an accident of language. Born when my mother's mouth
opened before it ought to have opened, born from her words
set free to my father. No bones with which to stand—
in a boat of reeds, I float and watch the camphor leaves
circle the bank. I cannot extend my arm toward their drift,
cannot dip a toe into the water that carries them.
At three, swaddled for the last time, mother kissed my cursed
forehead, placed me in the basket. So I float and still
I am nothing but eyes, ears, a nose, an angry throat. Nothing
but red honeycomb, deceitful softness of lungs—this wail
to the wind, this howl to the water—what happens
when the order is reversed, when the story is told out of turn.

The Birth of Athena

Her father's hands clamp against his skull. He is agony, a wilderness
of tremors, an underground river, fault line of molten scalp about to burst.
He is desert sand, gnawing white light. Someone is sharpening a blade
against steel. Someone is lifting the axe. Blood glistens metal,
the embryonic side of a girl in naked unfurling. A military beat swells:
right foot lifts, left foot falls. The cavern below his tongue fills with salt—
a single strangling curse—and a world rushes in to be. She, who emerges
solitary in a bead of blood, whose helmet dents the floorboards,
whose shield of folded goatskin shakes the cabinets square.
Her dagger. Gold. Silver. Sword. Spear. Iron. Her tunic. One by one
she drops her weapons, and they strike. He stares at the bloody wreckage
of his head, at his daughter, into her gray eyes that gut him.
Her two bare calves stepping over the heap, her bloodied sandal strap.

Elegy as the Veal Calf

If you are born into milk, if from the start you are only a barter,
if your body is the sweet scent of hay in the dark barn stall, snot dripping
from your snout, gloved hand on your flank ushering you from one pen
to another. If then your body is the cold pickup truck, wind through
the slats and the long drive, if then you hesitate and your hooves skid
on the ramp, if the floors are concrete and too clean to trust, if there is a man
with a hooked cane to see you across, if the air sours with threat but you
can only walk forward, if all you have to offer is the dumb meat and milk
of yourself. Know the thing they feel as they eat your flesh is called *love*.

The Calligrapher Tests the Daughter

A child needs to know she can kill her father
if she has to. My father says, *I keep my heart in a box beside my bed*
while I sleep. If you open the box I will die. He plucks one hair from my head
and places it over the box. Each morning he checks
to see what has moved—

Repetition Keeps Us Alive

I kill in my dreams. Someone old, body already tucked away
inside itself like a white blanket, prepared to die. Smother it
with a pillow. I do or you do. It's a mistake though;
we're filming a movie. We sneak out of the rest home
without being seen. We are interrogated later. We clean
the trunk for signs of blood. No one looks for us,
so we linger, camp out in a blue hospital room with only
one bed. Grandmother insists on sleeping in the wooden chair,
and I let her. Dried blood-splatters on my knuckles. My hands
splay across my lap. I don't know what I've done
but I am afraid for our lives, afraid of the silence. I wake
from nights, a wad of wet cotton. I hear your truck pull away.
I am sorry for everything. I call you on the phone and ask,
Who is buying the grain? Who is returning the library books?
I don't know why we keep having this conversation, you say.

In Western Calligraphy, an Act of Symmetry Forms the Letter *I*

I is the first letter: the twist of wrist. As a child I wanted to be hands
without arms. The gap between finger and thumb is a pen. Pure form
is air inside air. From the first, *I* was an imitation. Child-hand
creased at the palm, squared as the blank white page.
Every time: drop, narrow, pivot, widen, tear the paper, slur the ink.
I longed to be a stain in the snow: blood-webbed, distal. At eight,
I excised *eternity* from all my poems. But my father kept turning
pages, and I read every book he assigned me. I stopped
eating meat. I stopped eating rice. I smashed the window—
fist through glass, an essay on Macbeth. I lied about his face
slanting back. Done right, it's called *rotation.* I grip
the pen too tightly. Even then, I came to our story
through the bones in my hand.

In the Socket-Eyes of the Lungs

A snow not forecast: it falls all morning and does not stop.
I wear my jacket in the house, forget to eat. In the stove
fire rocks itself. I write and unwrite this poem, neglect
the chickens in their snow-sunk shack, water bucket frozen
or empty. Who can hear bird-cry in this wash of white. Relief
is the hollow under my tongue. The poet whose book
lies open in my lap says he found some light, some moment
before the gunshots, before the dog was left to die
in a field. Another word. I was born in an ink-stain dark river
to cracked palms, and if I could kiss you full
on your sawdust mouth, just once your barn straw limbs
would rise to dance your hackneyed rage, the numbest
among us in line for the show, praying with our ticket-stub lips:
let it grow, let it grow to some*thing,* let it grow.

Always a Mouth Wider Than My Own

Over snow gullets swelling hoarfrost teeth, it winds around the cabin,
braids through the woods. Over mud, skim-ice glinting the ditches
until the road below, and then all the yard, devours itself—my hill swallows
a neighboring hill, and the neighbor's car crawling slowly home beams brighter
than the coyote's eye hunting me out. The wind kisses its curled threat
around my neck. *How much longer until I am seen?*
Quick hands cinch tight this night made up of all our breath—

Full Hunger Moon

The hunter loses: first his steps, then his feet. And then his legs. And then
his way. Fear crystals the snow. At each trail of dropped teeth, the woods
lead him deeper. The task now is not to lose his body all together, to keep alive
this delusion of gristle and char, even as it mixes with the scent
of his own swelling. The hunter unfolds: a knife glinting in the pocket
of this night. The task now is not to let the moonlight
skin him bare. Somewhere a deer has bedded down in the white;
her heart beats an offering into the palms of the earth.
Somewhere his children are sleeping, three metal cups
in a neat row, waiting. Morning will find them
filled with blood or with snow.

Fear Visits the Calligrapher

If it comes belly-clawing up out of the woods, out of the bog, ready to lay.
If he leaves the basement door ajar while welding. If it is lured
by the soft sand ringing our house. If he finds it in a nest of his papers,
his *art,* and it hisses when she sees him and works her cigar-cutter beak,
and if he shrinks then, if he turns into himself, gray-faced, and flees,
calls the neighbor lady and demands, *Come with your gun,* and she comes

and shoots a turtle point blank in the face. If the snapping turtle's blood
stains the concrete pink. If her great battered carapace is suddenly gone.

Predator

Smell it before you see it: salivate before you know: ice spines
the blackberry canes: snaps bone against toothless night: against this throat-
torn night: this gut-turn night: smell it: how easily flesh becomes
thing: cools into dumb animal scent: how snow drops its fast blanket on this
woodlot night: black-bellied night: smell it: how *want* bends the mouth
so low you nearly kiss the ground.

Leukophobia

For nearly every human fear, we have names. Even our fear
of colors. In the dark I see your anger: red, yellow, white. The sheet is blue
as a gun, wrapping my throat. Our night room fills the gap of our turned
backs. Shadows. There is one above me now. How small
can I make myself become? You twitch your legs, so careful
not to touch. I'm hot and damp as a slapped child. The cat collapses
a shelf, and all the books fall purple to the floor. I know you are awake.
I will not close my eyes until I hear your breath hitch. Then,
the barred owl's four-point cry. Green slice of wing through sky,
gray clutch of claw to flesh. I fold my hungry hands into my chest.

Shriller Than All the Music

After Gaius Julius Caesar

For two days the parasite lives in his liver, then the chills. He's hiding
from Sulla's secret police—fever-soaked, on the lam. Arriving
after dark, the doctor finds him under straw in the barn, chaff-slicked
and trembling: a virulent case of Quarton fever. How easily is life reduced,
condemned to cycle—their suspicion keeps him on the run; every night
sleeping in a unfamiliar dwelling; every night a bribed farmer
or distant relative; every three days, the fever returns.

Who arranges the stalks this way? Who spills the entrails? Again and again
he returns to that city. And how many times did I to him, to the name
my father gave me—searching for a thread to trail the stone maze
of his stories: a destiny, a match-spark.
Every March 15th, I expected to die

because ambition dictates you must swallow everything
your parents give you, and then one day you must swallow them too.
Take his dream that night at Gades: her tunic creased at the back, sweeping
lock of auburn hair, pale shoulders, one hand around her throat
and the other on her thigh, his teeth in her neck before he hears
her familiar cry: she is his mother. Even then he does not stop.
The soothsayers tell him he will conquer
the earth. He, without limit.

Link arms in dark courtyards, build an army—any gladiator can tell you
how a dagger glints in the twist. It's only a betrayal if you don't
see it coming. Blood warbles his throat. Blood in his mouth.
Carry him out on that ivory couch and set him ablaze.

Elegy as Invocation for Ghosts

Hollow, I take to the woods road after dark, squat and piss
in the clearing under the open-mouthed moon, down
a bottle of stout while my little black shepherd forages—frozen apples
in the slash-field. Every shadow is a pile of rocks. Every rock
is an invitation for your hands to reach out and grab me
for lingering here—in this frozen wreckage, land hewn
of our spalting memory—I reach into my pockets to recall
the heat of my own flesh. *Tell me your name?*
I ask too loudly so you won't.

Arachne Spun

Because her father is a dyer, because her mother is dead, no one
but the wool tells her any stories. Now all twelve gods watch this girl—
who from her belly is spinning and spinning every shame and deceit
as if her fingers are discovering her fingers, as if her hands
are discovering her hands. She is thin as a distaff, in need of *anything*—
she plies the needle, she plies her tongue. Everything she touches
is transfigured to long threads—what is spun in the belly
or the mouth. Shuttle-struck is nothing but belly. She splays the wings
of the swan—weaves this tapestried girl, feather-branded skin tearing
white. And now she wants so badly to tell, she can't see what she's become:
her own red hour glass, her own black shine.

Night Light

Humans scent blood like dogs scent legs.
In the membrane room, you were the dark
of yourself curling into the dark of someone
else. Mother dreamed a belly of swallowed words;
in the morning, she washed her eyes with milk.
Go back. Father is hanging—he left a box full
of flesh-fingers, flesh-eyes inside the floor.
Sister is lighting a match in the bathroom mirror.
Two hands, a soft white thing against the bed.
Tap your bald spot twice. Take a story for luck.

Triptych

All objects leer from the edges of this room: sheen of menace swerving
corners, floor exhaling threat with every orange blue walls evade.
See the severed badger's head on the book stack, the swollen dwarf girl
on the wall. The dying are not dying; the well are not well.

If the room represents childhood, the two girls running or falling, naked
feet, thin cotton shifts—must be falling. The elder is suspended
as she trips air over floorboard over feet. The younger, neck twisted
in terror toward the stairway behind, doesn't see
her sister going down in front.

Because the painting is a child, it demands an answer: Will they fall?
Will they right their steps and run? Stare now at these
taxidermied: the next hallway beckons.
Floorboards mark the path—

Furrow the Tongue to the Throat of It

A steer hung from its hocks, stream of plasma under my boots,
water-thinned. The butcher works. Hands pale and firm. The steer hulks,
swivels shadow. The butcher opens him slowly. There are those who see
colors in numbers, those who hear music in bones. Cattle maddened
by the scent, buck-leap, brandish their horns, gore the ground.
Some people fear snakes, others fear ichor. Hens will rush the red bucket
first, and it's not the water they're after. Like kissing yourself,
blood congealed in a coffee can bears the shape of the coffee can.
I reach into the unwashed abdomen and recollect the breakfast table.
Again, I spread the cloth.

Elegy as First Red Hen

His body is stacked like cordwood into mine,
down crushing the weight of our silence,
his elbow's crook, an axe handle against
the winged moonlight of our bedroom wall,
his sleeping breath, a song on skin. I know
I must surrender to the black behind my eyelids,
but every night she's back again. Red hen, first hen,
red rusted bird—a slow rotation that sockets
open, circles out of itself, neck-twists back in.
She was beak-bright, pink as pain when failure came.
Then she became a soft belly, a stain in the sand
behind the scrub pines; a shadow, flannel plaid
blue into black, swinging arm and sharp step of work-
boot against spade. In this quiet room displaced,
let memory become the sacrifice my breath obeys.
Let her tuck her broken neck to sleep inside
her nameless breast. Let the child move her fingers
from her eyes. Now let the cracked corn fall
from the child's hand.

Sister, the Stomach

Sister, I long to hold this whole green world, to find us the water
that tastes like a desert mirage. So I squeeze the green speckled. I squeeze,
but a sickly white sac rises up, slides into the frog's mouth. It's the first time
my hands see my hands: this lockjaw love of mine, how it's always been here.
I stuff the stomach back, one finger. I palm a grave, patty-cake my shame
into wet sand, swallow this knowledge for us both.

Prey

All that's left of the shrew now is its track: breach you spot
in the gloved snow: secret grief you long to hold: how the cold-cupped air
of your palms swallows itself: a *C* for *cannot* that tunnels blindly
through winter's white mouth: perilous in the fact
of its own four feet until absence weaves the field tight
to the blackberry canes: wingspan against snow: scrambled finger-brush
as the hawk swoops low: the shrew's fear so invisible you could trace it:
your fingers a frozen keloid imitation of: always
only one way out and one way back.
See: how hunger leaves a crown of trailing breath.

Where I Am Now, I Find No Difference Between Tongues and Wings

My head is a bevy of black feathers, a thrashing against the pillowcase.
I think I speak to you, but I don't know if you are still in the room
sliding your belt on or if that click was the door shutting. All the birds
are lizards and the crows have teeth; a certain word can snap
just like a laundry line. I turn my other cheek to our ragged whipping.
I turn it so many times I cannot lift my head without wincing.
It's late. The dogs are barking. While I was sleeping the chickens
clustered on the balcony; the balcony became a fire escape.
I was in the park with Nanny. She was not dead. Her skin was birch bark.
Pigeons crawled toward us, and we threw lumps of stale bagel at them.
Her hands grabbed the tops of the trees, shook them out like paper bags.

Haying

There is no poetry in this work. Sweat flows spine like a river, drowns
blackflies in my waistband and chaff splinters fissure skin, arms, and chest
until my whole body is a burning barn. Words thicken a blanket
of storm clouds, a silence that hangs above our running limbs
until it smothers thought. The bales lie in the field waiting. The sky opens
its mouth to let its darkness out, and we know this moment only as *now:*
a counting off: one bale passed between six sets of hands, one bale pressed
into place beneath the eves, one truckload and another, our bodies
which cannot stop moving even as rain begins to beat its fists against
the barn roof, even as thunder sounds the pocketknife thrown
to the pile of sheet metal, even as bales spoil in the field until our bodies
lose the language for pain—until there is no before us and no after us.
The cat's eyes perch in the blackened barn, two kerosene flares waiting:
only the one more bale the cat needs to reach the swallow's nest.

The Calligrapher Practices Alchemy

The calligrapher rocks at the ledge, hairless white toes curled to the edge
of the roof, and his gaze—hawk-eyed, yellowing—swoops in and out
as heat and night tidal-wash over his skin. He shakes, hungry as a piece
of prey, empty as wingspan in the wide open air, waiting for the push.

By the time I am old enough to listen, he believes he controls time
with two pencils taped together. He tells me: *When I first pressed a pen
between my fingers, and it turned just as I wanted—my blood raced
with power.* He says: *Children are only one means toward my immortality.*

He says these words until it seems the possibility is born by the telling.
Membrane layered over membrane, his narrative is breach-born: a head
greased on its own words, pelvis splits like a hinge—a miracle. Say *push*
and the story pops out. And it will howl.

We take to the woods, sister and I, build a cave in the tall grass, build a nest
of rotten logs, line it with the hides of moles. In secret we show each other
our budding horns. Curled one across the other, in sleep we sweat the story
through our skins, fever it, rehearse in dreams what we'll one day resemble.

Our teeth grow sharper year by year—we bite our knees and lick our blood.
Soured fruit in jars, our goldfish laid in jewelry boxes. Our bottles of ink lie
uncapped and pooling. Any potion will do to collapse these sick white walls.
No matter what he does, his head remains cold as a cave.

The calligrapher pisses in the kitchen sink. Late afternoon light cinches
as the day's muscles stagger the spine. He is unable to gather strength to a
fist—for the first time certain forms cannot be made. A fragment hunched
over the punch of belly, a drunk hobbled by his blue jeans, he falls back
to the mattress, a rivulet of shit smeared on his thigh.

Then we tear the tattered pages down, burn our paper-airplane wings,

the singed masks of pounded onion grass, our hair and skin. We blot out
all the words with wax. We paint our faces with a lapis stare—blue
as a mouthful of swallowed air released in open falling. Tonight, we fly.

Elegy as Long Skin

I wind a ghost bracelet around my wrist, what the snake left for me
in the browning grass. I tack it to the window trim beside the fly strip,
sticky with buzzing, tiny legs kicking wings to sleep. Let this be the house
I live in forever—each passing fastened to my walls like paper.

My Questions Undress to Compare Their Scars

Most chimeras go through life without knowing they are chimeras.
Most marmosets are chimeras. I go to the doctor, and the doctor tells me
my liver is angry and my kidneys are sad. Who doesn't wish, just once,
to have the wrong DNA? Inside my head are a thousand walls, painted red.
Every betrayal is a different age, some older than the story I tell.
What if the lion devours the goat still attached, fear-eyed, to her back?
What if the snake mutinies? Poisons them both? Exterminates herself.
Cells woven through cells, a cross-stitch of fused fibers and no fingers
to untether the cords. I'll remove my cloak by bloodlight,
but still there is a chance you won't see. And if you do, remember:
the arrows pointing downward from my shoulders are only one
expression for you, my love.

The Calligrapher Builds a Faulty Oven

My father's head is an oven—heat that swells then shrivels.
The door to the oven is coal-smudged iron and cracked.
A unicorn guards the left; a troll the right, which is to say
they read me into existence. Which is to say *cleft*.
I broke down the door, it's true, but would I have been sorry
if his head had split?

My sister, my cousin, and me jumping on the hotel bed
with bottles in our small hands, beer spilling out our mouths.
Pity is a child's outstretched hand, the cicada shell still clinging.
I'd rather talk about revenge.

Instead we lie in the bed kissing our limbs, reading one another anew,
our upturned palms. What strange and wonderful beasts we are.
I am finally the happiest one. I taste the ash rising on my tongue.

Mercy for the One Who Sharpens

You rise praying each morning: *Mercy for this body*
climbing from its slow bed. Mercy for the ache
mistaken for joy. If the spine is a chipped blade,
if the hands are rusted axe-heads, *Mercy to the one*
who kneels for stove wood, to the pullet dangling
from her baling twine. Blood-rush eyes don't stop circling.
This is a lullaby. *Mercy in the bruised-mouth sky.*
How the tomcat butts his tattered ear against your face
and purrs thick and sweet as milk. *Mercy be to you*
who sharpens your blade.

After Another Dead Dog Dream

He snapped up a mouse, and I screamed at the tail lashing out
between his lips. This sleep fever is where my love has gone to burrow.
I awaken dry as a field in winter, starved for a swallow of sky.
Time becomes a lessening, and lessening becomes a thick down,
a white blanket that holds me here, even now, pins me to my bed.
I walk into walls. I pray to my toast: *May I never learn to be merciful to myself.*
Remember the crunch of tiny bones, his delight to devour something alive?
Crush it now, before the quiet. Squeeze it while it twitches.
That hollow between his eyes and nose where I used to rest my palm
is called *stop*—

This Friday Morning, Prayer

You wake me saying, *Get up. Get dressed. I need your help. Where
are the latex gloves?* Yours is a voice so calm my sleep-burned ears
mistake it for prayer. I dress for war. Jeans and muck boots, camo
bandanna tight. Blood on their flanks when I arrive at the pen, smears
so bright I think, *Fly bites,* but no—the red piglet in the middle
of the slop pan turns and his own asshole is hanging out of him, bitten:
the mouth-slicked sheen of a frayed cigar.

This is what I know how to do: hold on. You grab one back leg,
pass it to me, then the other, and we're in the dance, piglets screaming
and all I have to do is grip and *Don't let go,* take a step back, waltz,
try try try not to think about the wet splash on my lip
or how this must be what it's like to run a jackhammer,
and when your careful, blue-gloved fingers decide the tear is bad
and there is nothing more to be done, we hoist him belly up
into the pig shed. The others (curious, cannibals) trot behind,
rooting for a spill of blood or stale bread. Pig mouths
are questions that want no answers: only the grain pan.
We watch him eat and eat and eat. We watch him turn to waste.

Elegy as Dusk Rising in the Road

It's the fact of the ground. My arches braid
the arced ruts each evening, light blistering away
into droplets that fall from my eyelashes, unfurl my fingers
like breath into my sleeves. I know the way home
on this dark path as easily as I sense the crawl of legs
in the middle of a dream and reach, unthinking, to pluck
the tick's still-feeding mouth from my calf. At the next turn
I will crest the hill into the bald eye of your tractor—
its singular, cycloptic gleaming. You bend to pound
fence posts into hardened clay one after another
as a partridge instinctively drums his need
into the ground—this palpitation of flesh to land
a wing-beat that strings me feet to chest and folds
me, here, to our night road for just one more
long drink of our separately spinning shadows.

Foxes and Hens

The hens shrill us awake to the bullet dawn. Only animals move quickly
in such primordial light. My husband makes coffee with my rifle
in his hand. He goes to work, leaves it on the kitchen table for me to see.
Some days our hilltop is a balding arc of granite, something a girl
could hatch right out of. The fox, exquisite and brazen, takes two
in the broad day. I'm a lousy shot. The fox kills more than she can carry.
My husband ties two dead birds to a stake and waits. For a week
the hens summer-swell. I walk a wide circle around them as I do my chores.
The fox does not return. On Sunday, he drives their bodies
down the road and throws them to the trees.

As My Hair Braids the Noose

Summon every bird-cry or thump that stiffens me to gunmetal
in the dark barn—every solitary ritual that bends us to our knees at night,
palms clasped or open in surrender. I press seeds into dirt—only half
ever climb their way out. This maze of soil, tunneled dead end in my throat
is my bloodline. Give me your hand. Squeeze until I feel my own pulse
moan back; sister is plucking herself a monk's bald cap. My friend is drunk,
weeping while an invisible telephone rings in her bathroom;
her dead mother has something to say. I imagine eyes or cameras
everywhere, until there is no such thing as alone. Now, take my hand.
Squeeze and bless the body stumbling alive in its own haunting,
bless the breath that blasphemes back.

Elegy as Bonfire

Today I have clawed all the potatoes from the earth.
Today I have laid the garlic under the bed of soiled straw,
a last remnant of summer's hogs. I pull the fence stakes loose,
coil the wire shut. Our remains rooted up in ice-skimmed mud,
crushed leaves, sweet scent of their skins crumbling
under my boots. I stoke the logs as fast as they recede into ash.
Armful after armful. Smoke rises like a second breath.

Love Letter from Penelope

I weave silence in blackout corridors. Slices of sky, the heddle and reed,
caesura of my own breath falling on my fingers, the warp and weft
of your absence. My untying, a knot that slips and slips until
your death is a nest in my hands. I sit grief-carved in my wooden chair.
My suitors bang their cups, spit to the floor, demand. I do not hear them.
My burning mouth, no rain. I find a hair on your old tunic,
tie my finger until it purples, royal clot of our making.

The Art of Pulling Heart

Being a brute doesn't trouble you; a man must know how to think
as an animal. Say there is a snowy hill and a fox caught in a leg trap.
Say the fox is pulling against steel, panting pain-matted fur
into damp snow. Say the trapper comes stepping in snowshoes,
a quiet thudding through this thick white. Here your theory is clear
as twig snap. The trapper's wide and wooden foot descends. Catgut pins
the fox's red flank, as you clasp head and neck in your left hand
then slide your own snowshoe down over the hind legs. The heart
is just below the bottom rib: it jumps as your throat grip tightens.
Then, it's easy. The trapper feels it out, pulls until the cords split.
My love, would you do this for me—lay me down?
My brute, when the time comes, our hands will be so steady.

Dismembering

On the barn floor, three legs are bound with rope—the fourth, left free.
Two men drag the lamb to the ramp, roll it to its back. A third crouches
to cut. Dying is the shakes, flesh fights to get away. I see it under the fleece,
reduced to nerve and muscle, a couple of breaths. The lamb pants and shits.
Blood steams, congeals as it hits the steel tub. When the lamb kicks, I grab
the front legs. Back legs splayed, the knife severs hock, slits up a thigh:
first the left, the right. At the juncture of the two cuts, the front legs drop
limp. They fold when I let them go. A gambrel is an iron triangle:
two hooks at the bottom, a ring at the top. Hanging, upside down,
already half-opened, the lamb falls out of itself. We shouldn't have fed it
on slaughter day. Two of us to lift the stomach out. A cut down the middle
dumps half digested grass into the blood tub. The fleece and skin rest
on empty grain sacks laid out on pine boards. I bring salt and try to break
the clumps with my hands. Together, we unfurl membrane.
Together, we stretch and drape, it shines: a lace veil for the sun.

Elegy as Mud Season

Already the animal is softening. When I say my road is alive,
I mean mouths open up everywhere, spitting rocks, spitting bone

until one gives me a skull. I carry it up the path,
set it on the kitchen table. The canines are missing and the lower
jaw. But the eye-holes are so unmistakably round, we say *house cat,*
give it a name—this, our season for naming *loss*—

how it sifts off our skin, collects in soft mounds by the door. How it follows
us everywhere, even into bed where it sloughs the space between us,
grimed hollow parting our bodies in darkness warm enough
for a single, yellow blade of grass to grow.

Land and Body

Here, we have survived another year—take this bounty, our love,
the resistance we feel between our teeth as seeds crack
and extend their pale finger-selves into paper towel
then earth, buried alive so they may grow into green billowing
we will eat as a new promise, sauté in garlic, olive oil, feed
to one another as if to say, *There is no distance between taking
and giving,* a ritual of regret carried out beside the deer head
on the porch, its skin flaked to sodden leather, dark as leaf mulch,
and my hands have traced the pale, trifold stitching of skull,
and I have been in mud today, I have cleaned up shit, clotted
through boxes of frozen chicken—leg after leg split and stacked
like cordwood into the box, splintered bone, flesh skinned pink,
a cold meat—and your hands have set the cinderblocks for a woodshed,
have split the kindling, have dug the grave for the dog who lies
rotting against ledge-rock four feet down in a frost heave, waiting
until the irises spread up over his brindled, poisoned bloom,
his cancer-chewed paw, his canines shining white as the moon
that slips naked to run against our snow-spread lawn as we stand
in front of the door, your arms folding me into you
until I feel it, our hardness—the bicep and bruise of all
the sap buckets we have lifted and poured, every bag of grain hauled,
bale of hay thrown, animals we have mended and killed, tasted, tricked
to the slaughter, every potato forked from the ground, each nail
pounded, the boards above and below us—how all of it binds us,
grafts us, one into the other—our freshly harrowed skin.

Notes

"Out of the Lock Box"

Erichthonius was an early king of Athens and, according to tradition, half man and half snake. He was the child of Hephaestus and the earth (Ge), conceived when Hephaestus attempted to rape Athena. Although Athena successfully defended herself, some of Hephaestus' semen spilled onto the earth, impregnating her. Because Ge rejected the ill-gotten child, Athena adopted Erichthonius herself. In an effort to make the child immortal, she gave him a necklace with several drops of Medusa's blood and put him inside a chest. The three daughters of Cecrops were assigned to watch over the chest and warned never to lift the lid. Pandrosos obeyed, but Aglauros and Herse gave in to temptation and peeked; then, driven mad either by the sight of Erichthonius or by Athena, they threw themselves from the walls of the Acropolis. After that, Athena raised Erichthonius herself, often carrying him at her breast inside the aegis, along with her guardian snakes and the head of Medusa.

"The Leech Child"

Mention of the "leech child" can be found in the Kojiki, the oldest extant book in Japanese. Assigned to the task of procreation, the deity Izanagi-No-Mikoto and his wife Izanami-No-Mikoto were required to walk in opposite circles around a heavenly pillar before meeting to join in conjugal intercourse. When they arrived at the meeting point, Izanami made the unfortunate mistake of greeting her husband before he greeted her. Despite the bad omen produced by the woman's speaking first, the couple proceeded with the act of procreation. As a result, their first-born offspring was "a leech-child,' described in some versions of the story as having been born without bones. They placed the child in a boat made of reeds and let it float it away.

"My Questions Undress to Compare Their Scars"

This poem borrows text from the Wikipedia entry on chimera: http://en.wikipedia.org/wiki/Chimera

"Furrow the Tongue to the Throat of It"

Some of the language in this poem is adapted from *Inquiries into Human Faculty and Its Development* by Francis Galton (1883).

"The Art of Pulling Heart"

The title of this poem references a Native American trapping technique for dispensing with small animals without using a firearm. See: Martin Hunter's *Canadian Wilds* (A.R. Harding Publishing Co., 1907).

Acknowledgments

Grateful acknowledgment is made to the editors of the following publications, in which these poems first appeared, sometimes in earlier versions or under different titles:

Bellingham Review: "We Are Just Three Mouths"
Cider Press Review: "Foxes and Hens"
Cimarron Review: "Spell for Spring"
Colorado Review: "The Calligrapher Practices Alchemy"
Connotation Press: An Online Artifact: "For the Beaver Hanging in My Shed," "Sister, the Stomach," "Mercy For the One Who Sharpens"
Cutthroat: A Journal of the Arts: "The Leech Child," "Dismembering"
Hermeneutic Chaos Literary Journal: "Full Hunger Moon"
MEAD: The Magazine of Literature and Libations: "Elegy as Now"
Minerva Rising: "In Western Calligraphy, an Act of Symmetry Forms the Letter *I*," "Origin Story," "We Go on Vacation; the Calligrapher Stays Home"
Muzzle: "Elegy as Mud Season"
Natural Bridge: "The Calligrapher Tests the Daughter"
Pilgrimage Magazine: "Where I Am Now, There Is No Difference between Tongues and Wings"
RHINO: "The Calligrapher Builds a Faulty Oven"
River Styx: "Land and Body," "This Friday Morning, Prayer"
Salamander: "Furrow the Tongue to the Throat of It"
Still: The Journal: "When to Dispatch"
Weave Magazine: "Pariah's Call"
Whole Beast Rag: "Arachne Spun," "First Words"
Wisconsin Review: "The Art of Pulling Heart"

"The Art of Pulling Heart" was reprinted in *Be Wilder: A Word Portland Anthology.* Eds. Danielle LeBlanc and Emily Jane Young. Portland, ME: Pine Pitch Press, 2015.

Thank you to the Virginia Center for Creative Arts and the Vermont Studio

Center for residencies during which some of these poems were written.

This book would not have been possible without the incredible support offered by so very many, and I am deeply grateful to all of you for your insights, for encouraging and challenging me, for your mentorship and your friendship. Please know that though I have named only a few, I see each of you—you are embedded in my heart, my practice, my life, and within these pages.

I am particularly indebted to Penelope Laurans for first placing poems into my head when I was eight years old, and for remaining my longest and most faithful reader. To Kenny Fries for asking me the most difficult questions and never losing confidence in my ability to work toward them. To Joy Harjo and Pamela Uschuk. To Linda Pastan and Donald Revell. To Rebecca Gayle Howell. To my publishers, Ruth Foley and Caron Andregg, for bringing this book so beautifully into this world.

To my sister, Lexie Bouwsma, who carefully and lovingly read numerous drafts. To my partners in poetry, Meg Willing and Frank Giampietro, for the pints, the careful attention you poured into poems and manuscript drafts, and the hours of conversation both bawdy and earnest. To those friends who often know me better than I know myself. To my dear Millay Hill neighbors, past and present. To my family—

And most especially to Walker. The difficulties inherent in loving a poet have not escaped me. Thank you for standing beside me all these years, for supporting me and pushing me in equal turns, for your fearless honesty and relentless work ethic, for entwining my dreams with your own and nourishing them both. With heart and hand, land and body—this book is for you.